LINUX FOR BEGINNERS

The Comprehensive Guide To Learning Linux Operating System And Mastering Linux Command Line Like A Pro

LINUX FOR BEGINNERS: THE COMPREHENSIVE GUIDE TO LEARNING LINUX OPERATING SYSTEM AND MASTERING LINUX COMMAND LINE LIKE A PRO

First edition. November 27, 2023.

Written by Voltaire Lumiere.

TABLE OF CONTENTS

CHAPTER 1
INTRODUCTION TO LINUX

- **Understanding Operating Systems**

An operating system (OS) serves as the backbone of computer systems, orchestrating the communication between hardware and software components. In the realm of operating systems, Linux stands out as a prominent and powerful player.

Origins of Linux: Linux, developed by Linus Torvalds in 1991, was born out of a desire for a free and open-source alternative to existing operating systems. Torvalds, in collaboration with a global community of developers, created a Unix-like OS kernel that would evolve into the Linux we know today.

Open-Source Philosophy: At its core, Linux is built on the open-source philosophy, allowing users not only to utilize the system but also to inspect, modify, and distribute its source code. This transparency has led to a robust and collaborative development environment, where a diverse community continuously refines and enhances the operating system.

Distributions (Distros): One unique aspect of Linux is its diverse array of distributions, or distros. These variations cater to different user needs and preferences, offering a spectrum of desktop environments, package management systems, and default software. Popular distros include Ubuntu, Fedora, Debian, and Arch Linux, each contributing to the rich tapestry of the Linux ecosystem.

Advantages of Linux: Linux has earned acclaim for its stability, security, and efficiency. Its architecture allows it to power a vast range of devices, from servers and supercomputers to embedded systems and smartphones. The command-line interface, a hallmark of Linux, provides users with unparalleled control and flexibility, making it a favorite among developers and system administrators.

Community and Collaboration: One of Linux's defining features is its thriving community. Developers, enthusiasts, and users from around the world actively contribute to forums, mailing lists, and collaborative projects. This communal approach not only ensures continuous improvement but also fosters a spirit of shared knowledge and support.

In delving into Linux, one enters a realm shaped by collaboration, innovation, and a commitment to openness—an ecosystem that empowers users to harness the full potential of their computing experience.

- **Introduction to Linux and its History**

Linux, a Unix-like operating system, emerged in 1991 as a visionary project by a Finnish computer science student named Linus Torvalds. Torvalds, motivated by a desire for a freely accessible and collaborative operating system, began developing the Linux kernel. This initial kernel laid the groundwork for what would become a revolutionary force in the world of computing.

Open-Source Evolution: What sets Linux apart is its open-source nature. Unlike proprietary operating systems, Linux allows users not only to use the software but also to access, modify, and distribute its source code. This ethos of openness has fostered a global community of developers and users who actively contribute to the system's growth, resulting in a dynamic and adaptable operating system.

Diversity of Distributions: Linux's versatility is embodied in its distributions, or distros. These variations cater to diverse user preferences and needs, offering different desktop environments, package management systems, and pre-installed software. Notable distros such as Ubuntu, Fedora, and Debian have carved unique niches, contributing to the mosaic of choices available to Linux users.

Stability and Security: Linux has gained acclaim for its stability and security. It is the operating system of choice for servers, where reliability is paramount. The robust architecture of Linux ensures minimal system crashes and a resilient defense against security threats, making it an attractive option for mission-critical environments.

Command-Line Mastery: A distinctive feature of Linux lies in its powerful command-line interface. While user-friendly graphical interfaces exist, many Linux aficionados appreciate the control and efficiency offered by the command line. This interface empowers users to execute precise commands, automate tasks, and navigate the system with finesse—a trait valued by developers, system administrators, and power users alike.

Delving into the history of Linux unveils a narrative of grassroots innovation, collaborative development, and a commitment to principles of openness. This journey through time illuminates not just the evolution of an operating system but the spirit of a community that continues to shape the landscape of computing.

- **Getting Started with Linux Installation**

Choosing Your Distribution: Before embarking on the Linux installation journey, you'll need to select a distribution that aligns with your needs and preferences. Whether you opt for the user-friendly Ubuntu, the cutting-edge Arch Linux, or another distro, each offers a unique ecosystem. Visit the official website of your chosen distribution to download the installation media.

Creating Installation Media: Once you've selected a distribution, the next step is creating installation media. This typically involves burning the downloaded ISO file to a USB drive or a DVD. Many distributions provide tools for this purpose, such as Rufus or Etcher. Follow the instructions provided by your chosen distribution to create a bootable device.

Booting from Installation Media: With the bootable USB drive or DVD ready, insert it into the computer where you intend to install Linux. Restart the system and access the boot menu. The key to access the boot menu varies (common keys include F2, F12, or ESC). Select the bootable media, and the Linux distribution's installation environment will initiate.

Guided or Manual Installation: Linux installations often provide a guided or manual option. Guided installations are user-friendly and suitable for beginners, automating most configuration steps. For more control over the installation process, opt for manual installation, allowing you to customize disk partitions, select software packages, and configure user accounts.

Partitioning and File System Setup: Understanding how to partition your hard drive is crucial. Linux requires at least two partitions: one for the root file system ("/") and a swap partition. Depending on your preferences and system requirements, you may also create separate partitions for "/home" (user data) and other directories. Select the appropriate file system (commonly ext4) for each partition.

Navigating the Linux installation process is a pivotal step in your journey to mastering this operating system. By carefully following the distribution-specific instructions and making thoughtful decisions during installation, you'll lay the foundation for a stable and customized Linux environment on your system.

- **Navigating the File System and File Permissions**

Understanding the File Hierarchy: The Linux file system is structured as a hierarchical tree, starting from the root directory ("/"). Familiarize yourself with essential directories such as "/home" (user files), "/etc" (configuration files), and "/bin" (binary executables). Use the "ls" command to list the contents of a directory and the "cd" command to navigate between directories.

Pathnames and File Navigation: Mastering the use of pathnames is fundamental to efficient navigation. Absolute paths begin from the root directory ("/"), while relative paths are based on the current working directory. Utilize commands like "pwd" to display the present working directory and "cd" to change your location within the file system.

Basic File Operations: Become proficient in basic file operations to manipulate files and directories. The "cp" command copies files, "mv" moves or renames them, and "rm" removes files. Use "mkdir" to create directories and "rmdir" to remove empty directories. Understanding these commands is crucial for managing your file system efficiently.

File Permissions and Ownership: Linux employs a robust permissions system to regulate access to files and directories. The "chmod" command modifies permissions, allowing or restricting read, write, and execute access for the owner, group, and others. Learn to interpret permission symbols (r, w, x) and numeric representations (e.g., 755). The "chown" command adjusts file ownership.

Symbolic Links and File Paths: Linux supports symbolic links, which are shortcuts or references to other files or directories. Use the "ln" command to create symbolic links. Grasp the concept of relative and absolute paths when working with symbolic links to ensure accurate referencing.

Navigating the Linux file system and understanding file permissions are fundamental skills for any user. As you delve into these concepts, you'll gain the ability to organize your files, execute commands efficiently, and maintain a secure and well-structured Linux environment.

- **Essential Linux Concepts: Processes, Users, and Resources**

Understanding Processes: In Linux, a process is an executing instance of a program. The system relies on processes to perform tasks. Familiarize yourself with commands like "ps" to list active processes, "top" for real-time process monitoring, and "kill" to terminate processes. Processes are crucial for system management, and understanding their lifecycle is essential.

User Management: Linux is a multi-user system, and managing users is a key aspect of system administration. Learn the basics of user management with commands such as "useradd" to add new users, "passwd" to set passwords, and "userdel" to remove users. Understanding user permissions and groups is vital for maintaining a secure and organized system.

System Resources and Monitoring: Efficiently managing system resources ensures optimal performance. Use commands like "free" to check memory usage, "df" for disk space, and "du" to assess directory sizes. The "top" and "htop" commands provide real-time monitoring of CPU and memory usage, aiding in the identification of resource-intensive processes.

Job Control and Background Processes: Linux allows for job control, enabling you to run processes in the background or foreground. The "&" symbol can be used to run processes in the background. Learn to use "bg" and "fg" commands to move processes between background and foreground. The "jobs" command lists background processes.

Shell Environment and Variables: The shell environment plays a pivotal role in Linux interactions. Understand the concept of environment variables, which store information about the system environment. Use commands like "echo" to display variables and "export" to make variables available to child processes. Mastery of the shell environment enhances scripting and customization capabilities.

Grasping these essential Linux concepts—processes, user management, system resources, and the shell environment—lays a foundation for effective system administration and user interaction. As you delve deeper into these concepts, you'll gain insights into the inner workings of the Linux operating system and its versatile capabilities.

CHAPTER 2

MASTERING THE COMMAND LINE

- **The Terminal and Different Shells**

Introduction to the Terminal: The terminal, or command-line interface (CLI), is a powerful tool for interacting with a Linux system. Unlike graphical interfaces, the terminal allows users to issue commands directly to the operating system. Embracing the terminal enhances efficiency, enables automation, and provides a deeper understanding of system operations.

Common Terminal Commands: Familiarize yourself with fundamental terminal commands such as "ls" for listing directory contents, "cd" for changing directories, "cp" for copying files, and "mv" for moving or renaming files. Understanding basic commands forms the basis for effective command-line navigation and file manipulation.

Exploring Different Shells: Linux offers various shells, each with its unique features and capabilities. The default and widely used shell is Bash (Bourne Again SHell), known for its versatility and scripting capabilities. Other shells include Zsh (Z Shell) and Fish (Friendly Interactive Shell), each tailored to different user preferences and workflows.

Customizing the Shell Environment: Personalizing the shell environment enhances user experience. Configure the shell prompt, set aliases for frequently used commands, and customize colors and themes. The "/.zshrc" for Zsh) file contains configurations that persist across terminal sessions, allowing users to tailor the environment to their preferences.

Shell Navigation and Shortcuts: Efficient navigation within the terminal involves mastering keyboard shortcuts and commands. Use "Tab" for auto-completion, "Ctrl+C" to interrupt a process, and "Ctrl+Z" to pause a process. Explore the history of commands with the "history" command, and utilize keyboard shortcuts like "Ctrl+R" for reverse searching through command history.

Advanced Shell Features: Advanced shell features contribute to a more seamless user experience. Learn about job control with "bg" and "fg," piping commands with "|," and redirecting input and output. Understanding these features empowers users to compose complex command-line operations and automate tasks through scripting.

Diving into the terminal and exploring different shells is a gateway to the heart of Linux. As you become adept at navigating the command line, experimenting with various shells, and customizing your environment, you'll unlock the true potential of Linux's flexibility and efficiency.

- **Basic Command Line Operations and Utilities**

Command Syntax and Structure: Mastering the command line begins with understanding command syntax. Commands typically follow the structure: **command [options] [arguments]**. Options modify the behavior of a command, while arguments provide additional information. For example, **ls -l /home** lists detailed information about files in the "/home" directory.

Common Command-Line Utilities:

- **ls:** List directory contents. Use options like **-l** for detailed information and **-a** to show hidden files.

- **cd:** Change directory. Navigate to a different directory using the **cd** command followed by the directory path.

- **cp:** Copy files or directories. Syntax: **cp source destination**.

- **mv:** Move or rename files. Syntax: **mv source destination**.

- **rm:** Remove files or directories. Use with caution, as deleted files are not easily recoverable.

Redirecting Input and Output: Linux provides powerful mechanisms for input and output redirection. Use the > symbol to redirect command output to a file, and >> to append output to a file. Similarly, use < to take input from a file. For example, **ls > file.txt** redirects the list of files to a text file.

Wildcards and Regular Expressions: Wildcards, such as * (matches any characters) and **?** (matches a single character), facilitate working with multiple files. Regular expressions extend this capability for more complex pattern matching. For instance, **ls *.txt** lists all text files in the current directory.

File Manipulation and Permissions:

- **touch:** Create an empty file or update the access and modification times of an existing file.

- **chmod:** Change file permissions. Use symbolic notation (e.g., **chmod +x file.sh**) or numeric notation (e.g., **chmod 755 file.sh**).

- **chown:** Change file ownership. For example, **chown user:group file.txt** changes the owner and group of the file.

Pipes and Filters:

- **Pipes (|):** Connect the output of one command to the input of another. For instance, **ls -l | grep "file"** filters the list of files to those containing the word "file."

- **Filters (e.g., grep, sed, awk):** Process and modify text data. **grep** searches for patterns, **sed** performs text transformations, and **awk** processes structured text.

These basic command-line operations and utilities serve as the building blocks for efficient Linux usage. By mastering these commands, users gain the ability to navigate the file system, manipulate files, and perform a variety of tasks directly from the command line.

- **File System Navigation and Manipulation**

Navigating Directories:

- Use the **pwd** command to display the current working directory.
- Employ the **ls** command to list directory contents.
- Navigate to a different directory with the **cd** command followed by the desired path.

Creating and Removing Directories:

- Create a new directory using the **mkdir** command, e.g., **mkdir new_directory**.
- Remove an empty directory with **rmdir** or a non-empty one with **rm -r**, e.g., **rm -r unwanted_directory**.

Working with Files:

- Create an empty file or update access times using **touch**, e.g., **touch new_file.txt**.
- Copy files with **cp**, e.g., **cp source_file destination_directory**.

- Move or rename files using the **mv** command, e.g., **mv old_file.txt new_location/**.

Viewing and Editing Files:

- Display the contents of a file with **cat**, e.g., **cat file.txt**.
- Use **less** for a paginated view of a file, allowing easy navigation.
- Edit text files using text editors like **nano**, **vim**, or **gedit**.

File Searching and Filtering:

- Search for files or directories using the **find** command, e.g., **find /home -name filename**.
- Utilize **grep** to search within files for specific patterns, e.g., **grep "keyword" file.txt**.
- Filter and process text data with tools like **sed** (stream editor) and **awk**.

Symbolic Links:

- Create symbolic links with the **ln** command, linking one file or directory to another.
- Remove symbolic links using the **rm** command, e.g., **rm link_name**.

Mastering file system navigation and manipulation is fundamental to efficient Linux usage. These commands empower users to organize directories, manage files, and swiftly perform a myriad of tasks from the command line.

- **Advanced Command Line Techniques: Pipes, Filters, and Aliases**

Pipes (|) and Command Sequences:

- **Pipes:** Connect commands to create a data pipeline. For example, **command1 | command2** passes the output of **command1** as input to **command2**. This allows the chaining of commands for more complex operations.
- **Command Sequences:** Separate commands with semicolons (;) to execute them sequentially. For instance, **command1 ; command2** runs **command1** first, followed by **command2**.

Filters (e.g., grep, sed, awk):

- **grep:** Search for patterns within text. For example, **ls -l | grep "file"** filters the list of files to those containing the word "file."
- **sed (Stream Editor):** Perform text transformations on the fly. Use it to replace, insert, or delete text.
- **awk:** A versatile text processing tool that allows pattern scanning and processing. Useful for structured text manipulation.

Command Substitution and Variables:

- **Command Substitution ($(command) or `command`):** Embed the output of a command into another. For instance, **echo "Today is $(date)"** dynamically inserts the current date.
- **Variables:** Use variables to store and reference values. For example, **name="John"** and then **echo $name** displays the value of the variable.

Aliases:

- **Create Aliases:** Shorten and simplify frequently used commands by creating aliases. For instance, **alias ll='ls -l'** allows you to use **ll** instead of **ls -l**.
- **Persisting Aliases:** Add alias definitions to the shell configuration file (e.g., **~/.bashrc** or **~/.zshrc**) to make them available in every session.

Command Line Redirection:

- **Standard Input (stdin), Output (stdout), and Error (stderr):** Redirect input or output using **<**, **>**, and **2>** respectively. For example, **command < input.txt** takes input from a file.
- **Combining Output and Errors (command &> or command > file 2>&1):** Redirect both standard output and error to a file.

Understanding these advanced command-line techniques elevates your proficiency in Linux. By combining commands, manipulating text, and creating shortcuts, you gain the ability to streamline complex tasks and enhance your overall command-line experience.

- **Understanding File Permissions and Ownership**

File Permissions Overview:

- **Three Permission Levels:** Linux file permissions are categorized into three levels: owner, group, and others. Each level has read (**r**), write (**w**), and execute (**x**) permissions.

- **Symbolic Notation:** Permissions are represented in symbolic notation (e.g., **rwxr-xr--**). The first triplet is for the owner, the second for the group, and the third for others.

Changing File Permissions:

- **chmod Command:** Use the **chmod** command to change file permissions. For example, **chmod +x file.sh** adds execute permission to the file.

- **Numeric Notation:** Permissions can also be modified using numeric notation. For instance, **chmod 755 file.sh** sets read, write, and execute permissions for the owner, and read and execute permissions for the group and others.

File Ownership:

- **Owner and Group:** Every file in Linux has an owner and belongs to a group. The **chown** command changes ownership, and **chgrp** changes the group. For example, **chown user:group file.txt** changes the owner and group of the file.
- **Viewing Ownership:** Use the **ls -l** command to display ownership information alongside file permissions.

Special Permissions:

- **SUID, SGID, and Sticky Bit:** Special permissions provide additional functionality. The Set User ID (**SUID**) allows a file to be executed with the permissions of the owner. The Set Group ID (**SGID**) ensures that a file is executed with the group ownership. The Sticky Bit on directories restricts the deletion of files to the file owner.

Effective Permission Calculation:

- **Combining Permissions:** When a user tries to access a file, the effective permissions are determined by combining the user's individual permissions, group permissions, and others' permissions.
- **Access Control Lists (ACLs):** In addition to traditional permissions, ACLs provide more granular control over file access by allowing specific permissions for individual users or groups.

Understanding file permissions and ownership is crucial for maintaining the security and integrity of a Linux system. By mastering these concepts, users can control access to files, directories, and execute commands with precision, ensuring the confidentiality and integrity of their data.

CHAPTER 3

ESSENTIAL SYSTEM ADMINISTRATION

- **Role of System Administration and Common Tasks**

Introduction to System Administration:

- **System Administrator's Role:** A system administrator (sysadmin) is responsible for the configuration, maintenance, and overall operation of computer systems. Their role includes ensuring system security, performance, and reliability.

Common System Administration Tasks:

1. **Package Management:**

- *Task:* Install, update, and remove software packages.
- *Commands:* Utilize package managers such as **apt**, **yum**, or **pacman**.
- *Example:* **sudo apt-get install packageName**

2. **User and Group Administration:**

- *Task:* Manage user accounts and groups.
- *Commands:* **useradd**, **usermod**, **userdel**, **groupadd**, **groupmod**, **groupdel**.
- *Example:* **sudo useradd -m newUser**

3. **System Backup and Restore:**

- *Task:* Implement backup strategies and restore systems in case of failures.
- *Tools:* Employ tools like **rsync**, **tar**, or backup solutions like **rsnapshot** or **Bacula**.
- *Example:* **rsync -av /source /backup**

4. **Monitoring and Logging:**

- *Task:* Monitor system performance and analyze logs for troubleshooting.
- *Commands:* Use tools like **top**, **htop**, and review log files in **/var/log**.
- *Example:* **tail -f /var/log/syslog**

5. **Security Measures:**

- *Task:* Implement security policies, configure firewalls, and apply updates.
- *Commands:* Use **ufw** or **iptables** for firewall configuration. Apply updates with package managers.
- *Example:* **sudo ufw allow 22**

6. **Filesystem Management:**

- *Task:* Manage disk space, partitions, and filesystems.

- *Commands:* Utilize commands like **df**, **du**, and **fdisk**.
- *Example:* **sudo fdisk -l**

7. **Network Configuration:**

- *Task:* Configure network interfaces, assign IP addresses, and troubleshoot connectivity.
- *Commands:* Use tools like **ifconfig**, **ip**, and configuration files in **/etc/network**.
- *Example:* **sudo ifconfig eth0 up**

8. **Process Management:**

- *Task:* Monitor and manage running processes.
- *Commands:* Employ **ps**, **top**, and **kill** for process-related tasks.
- *Example:* **kill -9 processID**

9. **System Updates:**

- *Task:* Keep the system up-to-date with the latest security patches and software updates.
- *Commands:* Use package managers (**apt**, **yum**, etc.) to update the system.

- *Example:* **sudo apt-get update && sudo apt-get upgrade**

10. **Troubleshooting:**

- *Task:* Diagnose and resolve system issues.
- *Approach:* Employ systematic troubleshooting methodologies, review logs, and use diagnostic tools.

System administrators play a critical role in ensuring the stability, security, and functionality of Linux systems. By performing these common tasks and staying vigilant about system health, sysadmins contribute to the overall reliability of the computing environment.

- **Package Management: Installation, Removal, and Updates**

Introduction to Package Management:

- **Definition:** Package management is the process of installing, updating, configuring, and removing software packages on a Linux system.
- **Package Managers:** Different distributions use specific package managers, such as **apt** (Debian/Ubuntu), **yum** (Red Hat/Fedora), **zypper** (openSUSE), or **pacman** (Arch Linux).

Common Package Management Tasks:

1. **Package Installation:**

- *Task:* Install new software packages and dependencies.
- *Commands:* Use the appropriate package manager.
- *Example:* **sudo apt-get install packageName**

2. **Package Removal:**

- *Task:* Uninstall software packages.
- *Commands:* Utilize the package manager's remove or uninstall command.
- *Example:* **sudo yum remove packageName**

3. **Updating Packages:**

- *Task:* Keep installed packages up-to-date with the latest versions.
- *Commands:* Use the package manager's update command.
- *Example:* **sudo pacman -Syu**

4. **Upgrading System Packages:**

- *Task:* Upgrade the entire system, including the operating system and installed packages.

- *Commands:* Varies by distribution, e.g., **sudo apt-get dist-upgrade** for Debian-based systems.
- *Example:* **sudo dnf system-upgrade**

5. **Searching for Packages:**

- *Task:* Find packages by name or description.
- *Commands:* Use search options provided by the package manager.
- *Example:* **sudo zypper search packageName**

6. **Listing Installed Packages:**

- *Task:* Display a list of installed packages.
- *Commands:* Use commands like **dpkg -l** (Debian-based) or **rpm -qa** (Red Hat-based).
- *Example:* **sudo rpm -qa**

7. **Dependency Resolution:**

- *Task:* Automatically resolve and install dependencies required by a package.
- *Handled by:* Package manager during installation.
- *Example:* **sudo pacman -S packageName**

8. **Rollback or Downgrade:**

- *Task:* Revert to a previous version of a package.

- *Commands:* May involve using package manager options to specify a version.
- *Example:* **sudo apt-get install packageName=version**

9. **Repository Management:**

- *Task:* Manage software repositories to control package sources.
- *Commands:* Edit repository configuration files or use dedicated commands.
- *Example:* **sudo nano /etc/apt/sources.list**

10. **Offline Package Installation:**

- *Task:* Install packages on a system without internet access.
- *Approach:* Download packages and their dependencies manually, then transfer and install on the target system.

Effective package management is crucial for maintaining a well-functioning Linux system. Understanding these tasks and using the appropriate commands for your distribution ensures a smooth and secure software management process.

- **User and Group Administration**

User Administration:

1. **Creating Users:**

- *Task:* Add new user accounts to the system.
- *Command:* **sudo useradd username**
- *Example:* **sudo useradd john**

2. **Setting Passwords:**

- *Task:* Assign passwords to user accounts.
- *Command:* **sudo passwd username**
- *Example:* **sudo passwd john**

3. **Modifying User Details:**

- *Task:* Change user attributes like the home directory or login shell.
- *Command:* **sudo usermod options username**
- *Example:* **sudo usermod -d /home/newhome john**

4. **Deleting Users:**

- *Task:* Remove user accounts from the system.
- *Command:* **sudo userdel username**
- *Example:* **sudo userdel john**

5. **Viewing User Information:**

- *Task:* Display detailed information about a user.
- *Command:* **id username**
- *Example:* **id john**

Group Administration:

6. **Creating Groups:**

- *Task:* Establish new groups for users.
- *Command:* **sudo groupadd groupname**
- *Example:* **sudo groupadd developers**

7. **Adding Users to Groups:**

- *Task:* Assign users to specific groups.
- *Command:* **sudo usermod -aG groupname username**
- *Example:* **sudo usermod -aG developers john**

8. **Modifying Group Properties:**

- *Task:* Change group attributes.
- *Command:* **sudo groupmod options groupname**
- *Example:* **sudo groupmod -n newname developers**

9. **Deleting Groups:**

- *Task:* Remove groups from the system.
- *Command:* **sudo groupdel groupname**
- *Example:* **sudo groupdel developers**

10. **Viewing Group Information:**

- *Task:* Display details about a group, including its members.
- *Command:* **getent group groupname**
- *Example:* **getent group developers**

User and Group Management Tips:

- **Managing Home Directories:**
- When creating a user, use the **-m** option with **useradd** to automatically create a home directory.
- Ensure appropriate permissions on home directories to maintain user privacy and security.
- **Shell Access:**
- Specify the default shell for a user with the **-s** option in **useradd** or modify it later with **chsh**.

- **Bulk User Operations:**

- Utilize tools like **useradd** and **passwd** in conjunction with shell scripts for bulk user creation and password setting.

- **Group Membership Verification:**

- Use the **groups** command to verify a user's group memberships.

User and group administration is fundamental for maintaining a secure and organized Linux environment. By understanding these commands and tasks, administrators can effectively manage user accounts and group memberships on their systems.

- **System Backup and Restore Strategies**

Importance of System Backups:

- **Data Protection:** Backups safeguard against data loss due to accidental deletion, hardware failures, or system crashes.

- **Disaster Recovery:** In case of a system failure or compromise, backups facilitate quick recovery to a functional state.

Common Backup Strategies:

1. **Regular Data Backups:**

- *Task:* Regularly backup user data, configurations, and critical files.

- *Tools:* Utilize backup tools such as **rsync**, **tar**, or backup solutions like **rsnapshot** or **Bacula**.
- *Example:* **rsync -av /source /backup**

2. **Full System Backups:**

- *Task:* Create comprehensive backups of the entire system, including the operating system and installed applications.
- *Tools:* Employ disk cloning tools like **dd** or backup solutions such as **Clonezilla**.
- *Example:* **sudo dd if=/dev/sda of=/path/to/backup.img bs=4M**

3. **Incremental Backups:**

- *Task:* Perform backups of only the data that has changed since the last backup.
- *Tools:* Backup solutions like **rsnapshot** or **rsync** with the **--link-dest** option.
- *Example:* **rsync -av --link-dest=/previous/backup /source /backup**

4. **Snapshot Backups:**

- *Task:* Create point-in-time snapshots of the system for recovery at specific moments.

- *Tools:* Filesystem-specific tools like **LVM snapshots** or **Btrfs snapshots**.
- *Example:* **lvcreate --snapshot --size 1G --name snapshot_name /dev/VG/LV**

Backup Storage Options:

5. **External Drives and Media:**

- *Option:* Store backups on external hard drives, USB drives, or optical media.
- *Considerations:* Ensure sufficient storage capacity and safeguard against physical damage or theft.

6. **Network Attached Storage (NAS):**

- *Option:* Utilize network-attached storage devices for centralized backup storage.
- *Considerations:* Ensure secure access, regular monitoring, and redundancy.

7. **Cloud Backup Services:**

- *Option:* Use cloud-based backup services for offsite storage.
- *Considerations:* Choose reputable providers, encrypt sensitive data, and monitor costs.

Restore Strategies:

8. **Full System Restore:**

- *Task:* Restore the entire system from a full system backup.
- *Procedure:* Use disk cloning tools or backup solutions to restore the system to a new or formatted drive.

9. **File-Level Restore:**

- *Task:* Recover specific files or directories from backups.
- *Procedure:* Use file-level backup tools like **rsync** or extract files from archive backups.

10. **System Image Deployment:**

- *Task:* Deploy system images to multiple systems for consistent configurations.
- *Procedure:* Use disk cloning tools or deployment solutions like **Clonezilla** or **FOG Project**.

Best Practices:

- **Regular Testing:**
- Periodically test the restoration process to ensure backups are functional.

- **Automation:**
- Automate backup tasks to ensure consistency and reliability.
- **Encryption:**
- Encrypt sensitive backups to protect against unauthorized access.
- **Documentation:**
- Maintain documentation outlining the backup and restore procedures.

A well-designed backup and restore strategy is essential for system administrators to mitigate data loss risks and ensure the resilience of Linux systems. Choose a strategy that aligns with the specific needs and constraints of the environment.

- **Monitoring and Troubleshooting: Logs, Processes, and Issue Resolution**

Monitoring System Performance:

1. **Viewing System Logs:**

- *Task:* Examine system logs to identify issues and monitor system events.
- *Commands:* Use tools like **journalctl**, **dmesg**, and review logs in **/var/log**.

- *Example:* **journalctl -xe**

2. **Real-Time Monitoring:**

- *Task:* Monitor system performance in real-time.
- *Commands:* Utilize tools like **top**, **htop**, or **glances** for a dynamic overview.
- *Example:* **htop**

3. **Resource Usage Analysis:**

- *Task:* Analyze resource usage, including CPU, memory, and disk space.
- *Commands:* Employ tools like **free**, **df**, and **du**.
- *Example:* **df -h**

Troubleshooting System Issues:

4. **Identifying Processes:**

- *Task:* Identify running processes and resource usage.
- *Commands:* Use **ps**, **pgrep**, or **htop**.
- *Example:* **ps aux | grep processName**

5. **Process Management:**

- *Task:* Manage processes, including termination.
- *Commands:* Use **kill** to terminate a process by process ID (PID).

- *Example:* **kill -9 PID**

6. **System Resource Limits:**

- *Task:* Set resource limits for processes.
- *File:* Modify **/etc/security/limits.conf** or use the **ulimit** command.
- *Example:* **ulimit -n 4096**

7. **Network Troubleshooting:**

- *Task:* Diagnose and resolve network issues.
- *Commands:* Use tools like **ping**, **traceroute**, and **netstat**.
- *Example:* **ping example.com**

8. **Disk and Filesystem Checks:**

- *Task:* Check and repair disk and filesystem issues.
- *Commands:* Use **fsck** for filesystem checks.
- *Example:* **sudo fsck /dev/sda1**

Issue Resolution Strategies:

9. **Software Updates:**

- *Task:* Ensure software is up-to-date to resolve known issues.
- *Commands:* Use the package manager for updates.

- *Example:* **sudo apt-get update && sudo apt-get upgrade**

10. **Dependency Resolution:**

- *Task:* Address issues related to missing or broken dependencies.
- *Commands:* Utilize package manager commands.
- *Example:* **sudo apt-get -f install**

11. **Reconfiguration:**

- *Task:* Reconfigure software packages to resolve configuration-related issues.
- *Commands:* Use package manager commands for reinstallation or reconfiguration.
- *Example:* **sudo dpkg-reconfigure packageName**

12. **Service Restart:**

- *Task:* Restart services to apply changes or resolve issues.
- *Commands:* Use service-specific commands like **systemctl restart serviceName**.
- *Example:* **sudo systemctl restart apache2**

13. **Rollback:**

- *Task:* Roll back system changes to a previous state.

- *Approach:* Use backup and restore strategies to revert to a known-good configuration.

Best Practices:

- **Regular Monitoring:**
- Continuously monitor system logs and performance to detect issues early.
- **Documentation:**
- Maintain thorough documentation of system configurations and changes.
- **Training and Skill Development:**
- Invest in training for administrators to enhance troubleshooting skills.
- **Collaboration:**
- Collaborate with peers, forums, and online communities for issue resolution insights.

Efficient monitoring and troubleshooting are essential for maintaining a stable and secure Linux system. By mastering these commands and strategies, administrators can identify, diagnose, and resolve issues promptly, ensuring the reliable operation of their systems.

CHAPTER 4

NETWORKING IN LINUX

- **Introduction to Linux Networking**

Understanding Linux Networking Basics:

1. **Networking Overview:**

- *Definition:* Linux networking involves the configuration and management of network connections to enable communication between devices.

- *Components:* Includes network interfaces, IP addresses, subnets, and routing.

2. **Network Interfaces:**

- *Definition:* Network interfaces (NICs) connect the Linux system to a network.

- *Commands:* Use **ifconfig** or **ip** to view and configure network interfaces.

- *Example:* **sudo ifconfig eth0**

3. **IP Addressing:**

- *Definition:* IP addresses uniquely identify devices on a network.

- *Commands:* Set IP addresses with **ifconfig** or **ip** commands.
- *Example:* **sudo ifconfig eth0 192.168.1.2**

Configuring Network Connections:

4. **Network Configuration Files:**

- *Files:* Modify configuration files like **/etc/network/interfaces** or **/etc/sysconfig/network-scripts/ifcfg-eth0**.
- *Example:* **sudo nano /etc/network/interfaces**

5. **Dynamic Host Configuration Protocol (DHCP):**

- *Definition:* DHCP automatically assigns IP addresses to devices on a network.
- *Commands:* Use **dhclient** or configure the DHCP client.
- *Example:* **sudo dhclient eth0**

Network Diagnostics and Tools:

6. **Ping:**

- *Task:* Test network connectivity to a remote host.
- *Command:* **ping**.
- *Example:* **ping google.com**

7. **Traceroute:**

- *Task:* Trace the route packets take to reach a destination.
- *Command:* **traceroute** or **traceroute6**.
- *Example:* **traceroute google.com**

8. **Netstat:**

- *Task:* Display network statistics and active connections.
- *Command:* **netstat**.
- *Example:* **sudo netstat -tunlp**

9. **Nmap:**

- *Task:* Scan and discover devices on a network.
- *Command:* **nmap**.
- *Example:* **nmap 192.168.1.0/24**

Advanced Networking Concepts:

10. **Firewalls:**

- *Definition:* Firewalls control incoming and outgoing network traffic.
- *Commands:* Use tools like **ufw** (Uncomplicated Firewall) or **iptables**.

- *Example:* **sudo ufw enable**

11. **Routing:**

- *Definition:* Routing directs network traffic between different networks.
- *Commands:* Configure routes using **ip route** or modify routing tables.
- *Example:* **sudo ip route add default via 192.168.1.1**

12. **Virtual LANs (VLANs):**

- *Definition:* VLANs logically segment a network into isolated broadcast domains.
- *Commands:* Configure VLANs using **ip** and **vconfig**.
- *Example:* **sudo ip link add link eth0 name eth0.100 type vlan id 100**

Wireless Networking:

13. **Wi-Fi Configuration:**

- *Task:* Connect to Wi-Fi networks.
- *Commands:* Use tools like **iwconfig** or **nmcli**.
- *Example:* **sudo nmcli device wifi connect SSID password PASSWORD**

14. **Wireless Security:**

- *Task:* Secure wireless connections with encryption and authentication.
- *Protocols:* WPA2, WPA3.
- *Configuration:* Set up in network manager or configuration files.

Best Practices:

- **Security Considerations:**
- Implement security measures such as firewalls and encrypted connections.
- **Documentation:**
- Document network configurations and changes for future reference.
- **Regular Monitoring:**
- Monitor network traffic and performance for early detection of issues.
- **Backup Network Configuration:**
- Regularly backup network configuration files to simplify recovery in case of issues.

Understanding Linux networking fundamentals is crucial for effective system administration. By mastering these basics, administrators can configure, troubleshoot, and secure network connections, ensuring seamless communication between Linux systems and the broader network infrastructure.

- **Basic Network Commands (ping, ifconfig, etc.)**

1. Ping:

- **Task:** Test network connectivity to a remote host.
- **Command: ping**
- **Example: ping google.com**

2. ifconfig:

- **Task:** Display and configure network interfaces.
- **Command: ifconfig**
- **Example: ifconfig eth0**

3. ip:

- **Task:** Show and manipulate routing, devices, policy routing, and tunnels.
- **Command: ip**
- **Example: ip addr show**

4. netstat:

- **Task:** Display network statistics and active connections.

- **Command: netstat**
- **Example: netstat -tunlp**

5. traceroute:

- **Task:** Trace the route packets take to reach a destination.
- **Command: traceroute**
- **Example: traceroute google.com**

6. nslookup:

- **Task:** Query DNS servers to obtain domain name or IP address mapping.
- **Command: nslookup**
- **Example: nslookup google.com**

7. dig:

- **Task:** DNS lookup utility for querying DNS name servers.
- **Command: dig**
- **Example: dig google.com**

8. route:

- **Task:** Show or manipulate the IP routing table.
- **Command: route**
- **Example: route -n**

9. ssh:

- **Task:** Connect to a remote system securely.
- **Command: ssh**
- **Example: ssh user@remotehost**

10. wget:

- **Task:** Retrieve content from web servers.
- **Command: wget**
- **Example: wget https://example.com/file.txt**

11. curl:

- **Task:** Transfer data with URLs.
- **Command: curl**
- **Example: curl -O https://example.com/file.txt**

12. nmap:

- **Task:** Network exploration tool and security/port scanner.
- **Command: nmap**
- **Example: nmap -p 80 example.com**

13. arp:

- **Task:** Display or modify the Address Resolution Protocol (ARP) cache.

- **Command: arp**
- **Example: arp -a**

14. ss:

- **Task:** Show socket statistics.
- **Command: ss**
- **Example: ss -tun**

15. tcpdump:

- **Task:** Capture and analyze network packets.
- **Command: tcpdump**
- **Example: tcpdump -i eth0**

These basic network commands are essential for diagnosing network issues, configuring interfaces, and understanding network-related information on a Linux system. They provide valuable insights into network connectivity, routing, and communication

- **Configuring Network Settings**

1. Viewing Network Interfaces:

- **Command: ifconfig** or **ip addr show**
- **Example: ifconfig** or **ip addr show**

2. Configuring IP Address:

- **Command: ifconfig [interface] [IP_Address]**

- **Example: sudo ifconfig eth0 192.168.1.2**

3. Setting Default Gateway:

- **Command: route add default gw [Gateway_IP]**
- **Example: sudo route add default gw 192.168.1.1**

4. Configuring DNS Servers:

- **Edit Network Configuration File: /etc/resolv.conf**
- **Example: sudo nano /etc/resolv.conf**
- **Add DNS Servers:**

```
nameserver 8.8.8.8
nameserver 8.8.4.4
```

nameserver 8.8.4.4

5. Activating/Deactivating Network Interface:

- **Command to Activate: ifconfig [interface] up**
- **Command to Deactivate: ifconfig [interface] down**
- **Example:**
- `sudo ifconfig eth0 up`
- `sudo ifconfig eth0 down`

6. Configuring Static IP:

- **Edit Network Configuration File: /etc/network/interfaces** or **/etc/sysconfig/network-scripts/ifcfg-[interface]**
- **Example:**

sudo nano /etc/network/interfaces

Add the following lines:

```
auto eth0

iface eth0 inet static

address 192.168.1.2

netmask 255.255.255.0

gateway 192.168.1.1
```

7. DHCP Configuration:

- **Edit Network Configuration File: /etc/network/interfaces** or **/etc/sysconfig/network-scripts/ifcfg-[interface]**
- **Example:**
- sudo nano /etc/network/interfaces

Add the following lines:

auto eth0

iface eth0 inet dhcp

8. Displaying Routing Table:

- **Command: route -n** or **ip route show**
- **Example: route -n** or **ip route show**

9. Changing Hostname:

- **Edit Hostname File: /etc/hostname**
- **Command: sudo nano /etc/hostname**
- **Example:** Set the desired hostname in the file.

10. Network Restart:

- **Command: sudo systemctl restart networking** or **sudo service networking restart**
- **Example: sudo systemctl restart networking**

These commands and configurations provide a foundation for managing network settings on a Linux system. Whether configuring static IP addresses, enabling DHCP, or adjusting routing tables, these steps help ensure proper connectivity and communication within a network.

- **Firewall Configuration and Security**

1. Viewing Firewall Status:

- **Command: sudo ufw status** or **sudo iptables -L**
- **Example: sudo ufw status**

2. Enabling/Disabling Firewall:

- **Command to Enable: sudo ufw enable** or **sudo systemctl enable firewalld**
- **Command to Disable: sudo ufw disable** or **sudo systemctl disable firewalld**
- **Example:**

sudo ufw enable sudo systemctl enable firewalld

3. Adding Firewall Rules:

- **Command: sudo ufw allow [Port/Service]** or **sudo iptables -A INPUT -p [Protocol] --dport [Port] -j ACCEPT**
- **Example:**

sudo ufw allow 22 sudo iptables -A INPUT -p tcp --dport 80 -j ACCEPT

4. Denying Connections:

- **Command: sudo ufw deny [Port/Service]** or **sudo iptables -A INPUT -p [Protocol] --dport [Port] -j DROP**
- **Example:**

sudo ufw deny 23 sudo iptables -A INPUT -p udp --dport 5353 -j DROP

5. Removing Firewall Rules:

- **Command: sudo ufw delete [RuleNumber]** or **sudo iptables -D INPUT [RuleNumber]**
- **Example:**

sudo ufw delete 2 sudo iptables -D INPUT 3

6. Allowing Specific IP Addresses:

- **Command: sudo ufw allow from [IP_Address]** or **sudo iptables -A INPUT -s [IP_Address] -j ACCEPT**
- **Example:**

sudo ufw allow from 192.168.1.2 sudo iptables -A INPUT -s 10.0.0.1 -j ACCEPT

7. Blocking Specific IP Addresses:

- **Command: sudo ufw deny from [IP_Address]** or **sudo iptables -A INPUT -s [IP_Address] -j DROP**
- **Example:**

sudo ufw deny from 203.0.113.5 sudo iptables -A INPUT -s 192.168.0.10 -j DROP

8. Logging Firewall Events:

- **Command: sudo ufw logging on** or **sudo iptables -A INPUT -j LOG**

- **Example:**

sudo ufw logging on sudo iptables -A INPUT -j LOG

9. Firewall Reset:

- **Command: sudo ufw reset** or **sudo iptables -F**
- **Example:**

sudo ufw reset sudo iptables -F

10. Checking Open Ports: - Command: sudo ufw status or **sudo netstat -tunlp** - **Example: sudo netstat -tunlp**

Firewall Best Practices:

- **Default Deny Policy:**
- Set a default policy to deny incoming and outgoing traffic and explicitly allow necessary connections.
- **Regular Audits:**
- Periodically review and audit firewall rules to ensure they align with security requirements.
- **Minimize Open Ports:**
- Only open ports that are essential for services running on the system.

- **Use Application Profiles:**
- Utilize application profiles in firewalls to allow/deny traffic based on specific applications.
- **Network Zones:**
- Define network zones and configure firewall rules based on zones.

Configuring a firewall is a critical aspect of securing a Linux system. By following these commands and best practices, you can establish an effective firewall configuration that helps protect your system from unauthorized access and potential security threats.

- **Remote Access and File Transfer (SSH, SCP, SFTP)**

1. SSH (Secure Shell):

- **Connect to Remote Host:**
- **Command: ssh [username]@[remote_host]**
- **Example: ssh user@example.com**
- **Specify Port:**
- **Command: ssh -p [port] [username]@[remote_host]**
- **Example: ssh -p 2222 user@example.com**
- **Generate SSH Key:**
- **Command: ssh-keygen -t rsa**

- **Example: ssh-keygen -t rsa**

2. SCP (Secure Copy):

- **Copy from Local to Remote:**
- **Command: scp [local_file] [username]@[remote_host]:[remote_path]**
- **Example: scp file.txt user@example.com:/path/to/destination**
- **Copy from Remote to Local:**
- **Command: scp [username]@[remote_host]:[remote_file] [local_path]**
- **Example: scp user@example.com:/path/to/source/file.txt /local/destination**

3. SFTP (Secure File Transfer Protocol):

- **Interactive SFTP Session:**
- **Command: sftp [username]@[remote_host]**
- **Example: sftp user@example.com**
- **Upload File:**
- **Command: put [local_file]**
- **Example: put file.txt**
- **Download File:**

- **Command: get [remote_file]**
- **Example: get file.txt**
- **Navigate Remote Directory:**
- **Command: cd [remote_directory]**
- **Example: cd /path/to/remote/directory**

4. SSH Configuration File:

- **File Location: ~/.ssh/config** or **/etc/ssh/ssh_config**
- **Example:**

Host example HostName example.com User user Port 2222

5. Tunneling and Port Forwarding:

- **Local Port Forwarding:**
- **Command: ssh -L [local_port]:[destination_host]:[destination_port] [username]@[jump_host]**
- **Example: ssh -L 8080:internal-server:80 user@jump-server**
- **Remote Port Forwarding:**
- **Command: ssh -R [remote_port]:[destination_host]:[destination_port] [username]@[jump_host]**

- **Example: ssh -R 2222:localhost:22 user@jump-server**

6. Copying SSH Keys to Remote Host:

- **Command: ssh-copy-id [username]@[remote_host]**
- **Example: ssh-copy-id user@example.com**

7. SSH Agent:

- **Add Private Key:**
- **Command: ssh-add [private_key]**
- **Example: ssh-add ~/.ssh/id_rsa**
- **List Added Keys:**
- **Command: ssh-add -l**

8. Changing SSH Port on Remote Host:

- **Edit SSH Configuration:**
- **File: /etc/ssh/sshd_config**
- **Example: sudo nano /etc/ssh/sshd_config**
- **Change Port:**

Port 22 Port 2222

- **Restart SSH Service:**
- **Command: sudo systemctl restart ssh** or **sudo service ssh restart**

9. Disable Password Authentication:

- **Edit SSH Configuration:**
- **File: /etc/ssh/sshd_config**
- **Example: sudo nano /etc/ssh/sshd_config**
- **Change PasswordAuthentication:**

PasswordAuthentication yes PasswordAuthentication no

- **Restart SSH Service:**
- **Command: sudo systemctl restart ssh** or **sudo service ssh restart**

10. **SSH Tunneling for X11 Forwarding: - Command: ssh -X [username]@[remote_host]**

Example: ssh -X user@example.com

Remote access and file transfer using SSH, SCP, and SFTP provide secure and efficient ways to manage and transfer files between local and remote systems. These commands and configurations enhance security and streamline the process of remote administration and data exchange.

CHAPTER 5

LINUX SECURITY PRINCIPLES

- **Overview of Linux Security**

1. User Authentication:

- **User Passwords:**
- Passwords are stored in encrypted form in **/etc/shadow**.
- Password policies are defined in **/etc/security/pwquality.conf**.
- **Public Key Authentication:**
- Users can use SSH keys for passwordless authentication.
- Public keys are stored in **~/.ssh/authorized_keys**.

2. File System Security:

- **File Permissions:**
- Permissions are set using **chmod** (change mode) command.
- **ls -l** displays permissions for files and directories.

- **Access Control Lists (ACLs):**
- Extend standard permissions to provide finer control.
- Set using **setfacl** and viewed with **getfacl**.
- **File Ownership:**
- Owners and groups are assigned using **chown** and **chgrp**.
- **ls -l** displays owner and group information.

3. Firewalls and iptables:

- **Uncomplicated Firewall (ufw):**
- Provides a user-friendly interface for managing iptables.
- Enabled services defined in **/etc/services**.
- **iptables:**
- Command-line tool for configuring packet filtering rules.
- Rules are defined in **/etc/sysconfig/iptables**.

4. Network Security:

- **SSH Configuration:**
- **/etc/ssh/sshd_config** contains SSH server configuration.

- Disable root login and limit authentication attempts.

- **TCP Wrappers:**

- **/etc/hosts.allow** and **/etc/hosts.deny** control access to network services.

- Specify allowed and denied hosts or subnets.

5. Security Updates:

- **Package Management:**

- Update packages regularly with the package manager (**apt**, **yum**, etc.).

- Use package signing for package integrity verification.

6. Auditing and Logging:

- **System Logs:**

- **/var/log** contains system logs (**syslog**, **auth.log**, etc.).

- Monitor logs for security-related events.

- **Auditd:**

- The Linux audit framework allows tracking system changes.

- Configuration in **/etc/audit/auditd.conf** and rules in **/etc/audit/audit.rules**.

7. Process Monitoring:

- **top and htop:**
- Display real-time system statistics and running processes.
- Sort processes by CPU or memory usage.
- **ps:**
- Lists currently running processes.
- **ps aux** shows detailed information.

8. SELinux (Security-Enhanced Linux):

- **Enforcing and Permissive Modes:**
- SELinux can be set to enforcing or permissive mode.
- Configuration in **/etc/selinux/config**.
- **Context Labels:**
- Files and processes have security context labels.
- Display with **ls -Z** and **ps Z**.

9. Intrusion Detection Systems (IDS):

- **Fail2Ban:**
- Monitors log files and bans IPs with suspicious activity.
- Configuration in **/etc/fail2ban/jail.conf**.

- **Tripwire:**
- Integrity checker that detects changes to the file system.
- Configuration in **/etc/tripwire/twpol.txt**.

11. **Physical Security: -**

BIOS/UEFI Passwords: - Protect against unauthorized changes to system settings.

Boot Loader Passwords: - Password-protect the GRUB or LILO boot loader.

12. **Encrypted File Systems:**

LUKS (Linux Unified Key Setup): - Provides disk encryption for block devices. - Configured during installation or with **cryptsetup** command.

13. **Security Best Practices:**

Regular Backups: - Protect against data loss and facilitate system recovery.

Least Privilege Principle: - Users and processes should have the minimum necessary permissions.

Keep Services Minimal: - Disable unnecessary services to reduce the attack surface.

Linux security is a multi-faceted approach that involves user authentication, file system security, network security, system monitoring, and various tools and practices. By implementing these security measures, administrators can significantly enhance the robustness of their Linux systems against potential threats and vulnerabilities.

- **User Authentication and Password Policies**

1. User Account Creation:

- **Command: sudo adduser [username]**
- **Example: sudo adduser john**

2. Setting User Password:

- **Command: sudo passwd [username]**
- **Example: sudo passwd john**

3. Password Policies:

- **File: /etc/security/pwquality.conf**
- **Example:**

makefile

difok = 3 minlen = 8 minclass = 3 maxrepeat = 2 minclass = 4 maxclassrepeat = 4

4. Password Expiration:

- **File: /etc/login.defs**

- **Parameters:**
- **PASS_MAX_DAYS**: Maximum number of days a password is valid.
- **PASS_MIN_DAYS**: Minimum number of days allowed between password changes.
- **PASS_WARN_AGE**: Number of days warning given before a password expires.

5. Account Locking:

- **Command: sudo usermod --lock [username]** or **sudo passwd -l [username]**
- **Example: sudo usermod --lock john**

6. Account Unlocking:

- **Command: sudo usermod --unlock [username]** or **sudo passwd -u [username]**
- **Example: sudo usermod --unlock john**

7. Failed Login Attempts:

- **File: /etc/security/faillock.conf**
- **Parameters:**
- **deny**: Number of failed attempts before denying access.

- **unlock_time**: Time duration for which an account is locked.

8. pam_tally2 Module:

- **File: /etc/pam.d/common-auth**
- **Example:**

auth required pam_tally2.so deny=3 onerr=fail unlock_time=3600

9. Password Aging:

- **Command: sudo chage [options] [username]**
- **Example:**

sudo chage -M 90 -m 7 -W 14 john

9. **Force Password Change on Next Login:**

Command: sudo passwd -e [username]

Example: sudo passwd -e john

10. **Two-Factor Authentication (2FA):**

Tools: Google Authenticator, FreeOTP, Authy.

Configuration: /etc/pam.d/sshd

11. **LDAP Authentication:**

Integration: Configure **/etc/nsswitch.conf** and **/etc/pam.d/common-auth**.

12. **SSH Key Authentication:**

File: ~/.ssh/authorized_keys

Example: Add the public key to the file.

13. **System-wide Authentication Configuration:**

File: /etc/security/access.conf

Example: -:ALL EXCEPT root (admin):ALL

14. **Password History:**

File: /etc/security/opasswd

Configuration: /etc/security/pam_unix.conf

15. **Kerberos Authentication:**

Integration: Configure **/etc/krb5.conf** and **/etc/pam.d/common-auth**.

16. **Biometric Authentication:**

Hardware: Fingerprint readers, face recognition.

Configuration: Varies by hardware and software.

17. **Pluggable Authentication Modules (PAM):**

Configuration Files: /etc/pam.d/*

Example: Configure **/etc/pam.d/common-auth** for common authentication settings.

Implementing robust user authentication and password policies is crucial for securing Linux systems. By combining various tools, configurations, and practices, administrators can establish a strong defense against unauthorized access and enhance the overall security posture of the system.

- **File and Directory Permissions for Security**

1. Understanding Permissions:

- **Command: ls -l** for detailed listing.
- **Example:**

-rwxr-x--- 1 user group 1024 Nov 10 12:00 myfile

2. Changing Permissions:

- **Command: chmod [permissions] [file/directory]**
- **Example: chmod 755 myfile**

3. File Ownership:

- **Command: chown [owner]:[group] [file/directory]**
- **Example: chown john:staff myfile**

4. File and Directory Permissions:

- **Symbolic Notation:**
- **r** - Read
- **w** - Write
- **x** - Execute
- **Numeric Notation:**
- **4** - Read
- **2** - Write
- **1** - Execute
- **Example:**

-rwxr-x--- (Owner: rwx, Group: r-x, Others: ---)

5. Default Permissions:

- **umask Command:**
- **umask** sets default permissions for newly created files and directories.
- **Example: umask 027** (Results in default permissions of 640 for files and 750 for directories.)

6. Special Permissions:

- **Setuid (s):**
- Allows a user to execute a file with the permissions of the file owner.
- **Example: chmod u+s myfile**
- **Setgid (g):**
- Allows a user to inherit the group ownership of the directory.
- **Example: chmod g+s mydirectory**
- **Sticky Bit (t):**
- Restricts the deletion of files in a directory to the file owner.
- **Example: chmod +t mydirectory**

7. Access Control Lists (ACLs):

- **Command: setfacl** to set ACL, **getfacl** to view ACL.
- **Example:**

setfacl -m u:jane:rw myfile

8. Directory Permissions:

- **Read (r):**
- Allows listing of files in the directory.

- **Write (w):**
- Allows creating, deleting, or renaming files in the directory.
- **Execute (x):**
- Allows access to files and subdirectories within the directory.

9. Best Practices:

- **Principle of Least Privilege:**
- Assign the minimum necessary permissions to users and groups.
- **Regular Audits:**
- Periodically review and update permissions.
- **Separation of Duties:**
- Differentiate between users with different responsibilities.
- **Protecting Sensitive Files:**
- Set restrictive permissions on files containing sensitive information.

11. **File and Directory Ownership:**

Root Ownership: - Critical system files should be owned by the root user.

Regular User Ownership: - Users should own their home directories and non-system files.

12. **SELinux Context Labels:**

Command: ls -Z to view context labels.

Example: chcon -t httpd_sys_content_t index.html

13. **File Attributes:**

Command: chattr to set or remove file attributes.

Example: chattr +i myfile (Sets the immutable attribute.)

14. **Encryption:**

LUKS for Disk Encryption: - Encrypt sensitive data at the disk level.

Example: cryptsetup luksFormat /dev/sdb1

15. **Monitoring and Logging:**

Auditd: - Monitor changes to file permissions and ownership.

Example: auditctl -w /path/to/file -p w -k file_change

File and directory permissions are fundamental to Linux security. Properly configuring permissions, ownership, and additional security features contribute to a robust access control mechanism, ensuring that users have the appropriate level of access while minimizing potential security risks.

- **Securing Network Services**

1. Unnecessary Service Removal:

- **Command to Disable Service: sudo systemctl disable [service]**
- **Example: sudo systemctl disable telnet**

2. Firewall Configuration:

- **Uncomplicated Firewall (ufw):**
  - **Command to Allow Port: sudo ufw allow [port]**
  - **Example: sudo ufw allow 22**
- **iptables:**
  - **Command to Allow Port: sudo iptables -A INPUT -p [protocol] --dport [port] -j ACCEPT**
  - **Example: sudo iptables -A INPUT -p tcp --dport 80 -j ACCEPT**

3. Secure Shell (SSH) Configuration:

- **File: /etc/ssh/sshd_config**
  - Disable root login: **PermitRootLogin no**
  - Change default port: **Port [new_port]**
  - Allow specific users: **AllowUsers [username]**

- Disable password authentication: **PasswordAuthentication no**

4. Host-Based Access Control (TCP Wrappers):

- **Files: /etc/hosts.allow** and **/etc/hosts.deny**
- **Example:**

sshd: 192.168.1. ALL: ALL

5. Network Port Scanning Prevention:

- **File: /etc/sysctl.conf**
- **Configuration: net.ipv4.tcp_syncookies = 1**

6. Network Service Hardening:

- **Web Server (Apache):**
- Disable directory listing: **Options -Indexes**
- Limit request size: **LimitRequestBody 102400**
- **Database Server (MySQL):**
- Remove anonymous users: **DROP USER ''@'localhost';**
- Disable remote root login: **DELETE FROM mysql.user WHERE User='root' AND Host NOT IN ('localhost', '127.0.0.1', '::1');**

7. Intrusion Detection and Prevention:

- **Fail2Ban:**
- Monitor logs and ban IP addresses with multiple failed login attempts.
- **Example: sudo apt-get install fail2ban**

8. SSL/TLS Configuration:

- **Web Server (Apache):**
- Use strong ciphers: **SSLCipherSuite HIGH:MEDIUM:!aNULL:!MD5:!SEED:!IDEA**
- Enable HSTS: **Header always set Strict-Transport-Security "max-age=31536000; includeSubDomains; preload"**
- **Mail Server (Postfix):**
- Enable TLS: **smtpd_tls_security_level = may**

9. DNS Security (DNSSEC):

- **File: /etc/bind/named.conf.options**
- **Configuration: dnssec-validation auto;**

11. **Virtual Private Network (VPN) Security:**

OpenVPN: - Use strong encryption algorithms.

Example: cipher AES-256-CBC - IPsec: - Configure IPsec policies and key exchange methods.

12. **Web Application Security:**

Web Application Firewall (WAF): - Use WAF to protect against common web application attacks.

Example: ModSecurity with Apache.

13. **Regular Software Updates:**

Command: sudo apt update && sudo apt upgrade

Example: Keep all software and services up to date to patch security vulnerabilities.

14. **Log Management:**

Centralized Logging: - Use tools like syslog or ELK stack for centralized log management.

Log Rotation: - Configure log rotation to prevent log files from consuming excessive disk space.

15. **Network Service Monitoring:**

Intrusion Detection Systems (IDS): - Implement IDS tools like Snort or Suricata to monitor network traffic.

Port Monitoring: - Regularly review open ports with tools like **netstat** or **nmap**.

16. **Secure File Transfer Protocols:**

SCP and SFTP: - Prefer secure file transfer protocols over unencrypted alternatives. - Use SSH keys for authentication.

Securing network services involves a combination of configuration settings, access controls, encryption, and regular maintenance. Implementing these measures helps protect against unauthorized access, network attacks, and potential security vulnerabilities in various services running on a Linux system.

- **Security Best Practices and Auditing Tools**

1. Regular Software Updates:

- **Command: sudo apt update && sudo apt upgrade**
- **Best Practice:** Keep all software and packages up to date to patch security vulnerabilities.

2. Principle of Least Privilege:

- **Best Practice:** Limit user and system access to the minimum required for tasks.

3. Strong Password Policies:

- **File: /etc/security/pwquality.conf**
- **Best Practice:** Enforce password complexity and expiration.

4. Network Segmentation:

- **Best Practice:** Isolate sensitive network segments to contain potential breaches.

5. Intrusion Detection Systems (IDS):

- **Tool:** Snort, Suricata
- **Best Practice:** Implement IDS to monitor and detect suspicious network activity.

6. Log Management:

- **Centralized Logging:**
- **Tool:** syslog, ELK stack
- **Best Practice:** Centralize logs for analysis and monitoring.

7. Regular Security Audits:

- **Tool:** Lynis, OpenVAS
- **Best Practice:** Conduct periodic security audits to identify vulnerabilities.

8. File Integrity Checking:

- **Tool:** Tripwire, AIDE
- **Best Practice:** Monitor file integrity to detect unauthorized changes.

9. SELinux (Security-Enhanced Linux):

- **Best Practice:** Enable SELinux for additional access controls.

11. **Two-Factor Authentication (2FA):**

Tools: Google Authenticator, FreeOTP

Best Practice: Enhance authentication with 2FA for critical accounts.

12. **Disable Unnecessary Services:**

Best Practice: Disable unused services to reduce the attack surface.

13. **Encryption:**

Best Practice: Use encryption for data in transit (SSL/TLS) and data at rest (LUKS).

14. **Regular Backups:**

Best Practice: Schedule regular backups to prevent data loss in case of a security incident.

15. **Security Training and Awareness:**

Best Practice: Educate users and staff about security best practices and common threats.

16. **Physical Security:**

Best Practice: Secure physical access to servers and networking equipment.

17. **Disable Root Login:**

Best Practice: Prohibit direct root login via SSH for enhanced security.

18. **Restricting Network Access:**

Best Practice: Use firewalls and access control lists to limit network exposure.

19. **Use Secure Protocols:**

Best Practice: Prefer secure protocols (SSH, HTTPS) over insecure alternatives.

20. **Security Policies and Procedures:**

Best Practice: Establish and enforce security policies and procedures.

21. **Regular Security Training:**

Best Practice: Keep IT staff and users informed about the latest security threats and techniques.

22. **Incident Response Plan:**

Best Practice: Develop and maintain an incident response plan for quick and effective responses to security incidents.

23. **Access Reviews:**

Best Practice: Regularly review and revoke unnecessary user access to systems and data.

24. **Security Patch Management:**

Best Practice: Implement a systematic approach to applying security patches promptly.

Implementing security best practices and using auditing tools contribute to a robust security posture, helping to prevent, detect, and respond to potential security threats effectively. Regular assessments and proactive measures are essential components of maintaining a secure and resilient IT environment.

CHAPTER 6

SHELL SCRIPTING AND AUTOMATION

- **Introduction to Shell Scripting**

1. What is Shell Scripting?

- **Definition:**
- Shell scripting involves writing a series of commands in a script file to be executed by the Unix/Linux shell.
- **Purpose:**
- Automation of repetitive tasks.
- Batch processing and system administration.
- Creating custom utilities and tools.

2. Types of Shells:

- **Bourne Shell (sh):**
- Original Unix shell.
- **Bash (Bourne Again Shell):**
- Enhanced version of the Bourne Shell, widely used on Linux systems.
- **Zsh (Z Shell):**
- Extended features and improved user interface.

3. Writing Your First Shell Script:

- **Create a Script:**
- Use a text editor (e.g., **nano**, **vim**, **gedit**) to create a script file.
- Save with a **.sh** extension.
- **Shebang Line:**
- Start the script with **#!/bin/bash** to specify the shell.
- **Example Script:**

#!/bin/bash echo "Hello, World!"

4. Running a Shell Script:

- **Permission:**
- Make the script executable using **chmod +x script.sh**.
- **Execution:**
- Run the script using **./script.sh** or **bash script.sh**.

5. Variables and Data Types:

- **Variable Assignment:**

name="John" age=25

- **Usage:**

echo "Name: $name" echo "Age: $age"

6. Input from Users:

- **Read Command:**

echo "Enter your name:" read username echo "Hello, $username!"

7. Conditional Statements:

- **If Statement:**

if ["$age" -ge 18]; then echo "You are an adult." else echo "You are a minor." fi

8. Loops:

- **For Loop:**

for i in {1..5}; do echo "Number: $i" done

- **While Loop:**

count=1 while [$count -le 5]; do echo "Count: $count" ((count++)) done

9. Functions:

- **Define a Function:**

greet() { echo "Hello, $1!" }

- **Call the Function:**

greet "Alice"

10. Scripting Best Practices:

- **Comments:**
- Use comments to explain complex sections.
- **Indentation:**
- Maintain consistent indentation for readability.
- **Error Handling:**
- Implement error checking and handling.
- **Modularity:**
- Break down scripts into functions for reusability.

11. Real-world Examples:

- **Backup Script:**
- Automate the backup of important files.
- **System Monitoring:**
- Create a script to check system resource usage.
- **Log Analysis:**
- Parse and analyze log files for specific events.

Shell scripting is a powerful tool for automating tasks, system administration, and customizing workflows on Unix/Linux systems. Learning the basics provides a foundation for creating efficient and automated solutions in a command-line environment.

- **Writing and Running Shell Scripts**

Writing and Running Shell Scripts

1. Creating a Shell Script:

- **Using a Text Editor:**
- Open a text editor like **nano**, **vim**, or **gedit**.
- Create a new file and save it with a **.sh** extension.
- **Example Script (myscript.sh):**

bash

#!/bin/bash # This is a simple shell script echo "Hello, world!"

2. Making the Script Executable:

- **Command:**

bash

chmod +x myscript.sh

- **Explanation:**
- **chmod** changes file permissions.
- **+x** adds execute permission.
- Now, the script can be executed.

3. Running the Shell Script:

- **Command:**

bashCopy code

./myscript.sh

- **Explanation:**
- Use **./** to run a script in the current directory.
- Alternatively, you can use **bash myscript.sh**.

4. Variables and Input:

- **Example Script (input_example.sh):**

#!/bin/bash echo "Enter your name:" read name echo "Enter your age:" read age echo "Hello, $name! You are $age years old."

5. Conditional Statements:

- **Example Script (conditional_example.sh):**

#!/bin/bash echo "Enter a number:" read number if [$number -gt 0]; then echo "The number is positive." elif [$number -lt 0]; then echo "The number is negative." else echo "The number is zero." fi

6. Loops:

- **Example Script (loop_example.sh):**

#!/bin/bash echo "Using for loop:" for i in {1..5}; do echo "Number: $i" done echo "Using while loop:" count=1 while [$count -le 5]; do echo "Count: $count" ((count++)) done

7. Functions:

- **Example Script (function_example.sh):**

#!/bin/bash greet() { echo "Hello, $1!" } greet "Alice"

8. Command-Line Arguments:

- **Example Script (arguments_example.sh):**

#!/bin/bash echo "Script Name: $0" echo "First Argument: $1" echo "Second Argument: $2"

9. Error Handling:

- **Example Script (error_handling.sh):**

#!/bin/bash if [$# -eq 0]; then echo "Error: No arguments provided." exit 1 fi echo "Arguments provided: $@"

10. Script Best Practices:

- **Comments:**
- Use comments to explain complex sections.
- **Indentation:**
- Maintain consistent indentation for readability.
- **Error Handling:**
- Implement error checking and handling.
- **Modularity:**
- Break down scripts into functions for reusability.

11. Real-world Examples:

- **Backup Script:**
- Automate the backup of important files.
- **System Monitoring:**
- Create a script to check system resource usage.
- **Log Analysis:**
- Parse and analyze log files for specific events.

Writing and running shell scripts provide a powerful way to automate tasks, enhance system administration, and customize workflows on Unix/Linux systems. As you become familiar with shell scripting, you can create efficient and tailored solutions to meet specific requirements.

- **Conditional Statements and Loops**

1. If Statements:

- **Syntax:**

if [condition]; then # Code to execute if the condition is true elif [another_condition]; then # Code to execute if the second condition is true else # Code to execute if none of the conditions are true fi

- **Example (if_example.sh):**

#!/bin/bash echo "Enter a number:" read number if [$number -gt 0]; then echo "The number is positive." elif [$number -lt 0];

then echo "The number is negative." else echo "The number is zero." fi

2. For Loops:

- **Syntax:**

for variable in {start..end..increment}; do # Code to execute in each iteration done

- **Example (for_loop_example.sh):**

#!/bin/bash echo "Using for loop:" for i in {1..5}; do echo "Number: $i" done

3. While Loops:

- **Syntax:**

while [condition]; do # Code to execute as long as the condition is true done

- **Example (while_loop_example.sh):**

#!/bin/bash echo "Using while loop:" count=1 while [$count -le 5]; do echo "Count: $count" ((count++)) done

4. Until Loops:

- **Syntax:**

until [condition]; do # Code to execute until the condition becomes true done

- **Example (until_loop_example.sh):**

#!/bin/bash echo "Using until loop:" count=1 until [$count -gt 5]; do echo "Count: $count" ((count++)) done

5. Select Loop:

- **Syntax:**

select variable in option1 option2 option3; do # Code to execute based on the selected option done

- **Example (select_loop_example.sh):**

#!/bin/bash PS3="Select a color: " select color in Red Green Blue Quit; do case $color in Red) echo "You chose Red." ;; Green) echo "You chose Green." ;; Blue) echo "You chose Blue." ;; Quit) echo "Exiting." break ;; *) echo "Invalid option." ;; esac done

6. Break and Continue:

- **Break:**
- Terminates the loop.
- Example (**break_example.sh**):

#!/bin/bash for i in {1..10}; do echo "Number: $i" if [$i -eq 5]; then echo "Breaking the loop." break fi done

- **Continue:**
- Skips the rest of the loop code and moves to the next iteration.

- Example (**continue_example.sh**):

#!/bin/bash for i in {1..5}; do if [$i -eq 3]; then echo "Skipping iteration $i." continue fi echo "Number: $i" done

Conditional statements and loops are fundamental building blocks in shell scripting, providing the ability to make decisions and repeat actions based on specific conditions. By mastering these constructs, you can create powerful and flexible scripts to automate various tasks on Unix/Linux systems.

- **Functions and Variables in Shell Scripts**

1. Variables:

- **Definition:**
- Variables store data values in shell scripts.
- Variable names are case-sensitive.
- **Example (variables_example.sh):**

#!/bin/bash # Variable assignment greeting="Hello, world!" number=42 # Variable usage echo $greeting echo "The answer is $number."

2. User Input:

- **Reading User Input:**

#!/bin/bash echo "Enter your name:" read username echo "Hello, $username!"

3. Local and Global Variables:

- **Local Variables:**
- Defined within a function and have local scope.
- Example (**local_variable_example.sh**):

#!/bin/bash my_function() { local local_variable="Local variable" echo $local_variable } my_function # Attempting to echo $local_variable outside the function will result in an error.

- **Global Variables:**
- Defined outside functions and have global scope.
- Example (**global_variable_example.sh**):

#!/bin/bash global_variable="Global variable" my_function() { echo $global_variable } my_function # You can access $global_variable outside the function.

4. Functions:

- **Function Definition:**

function my_function() { # Function code here }

- **Function Call:**

my_function

- **Example (function_example.sh):**

#!/bin/bash greet() { echo "Hello, $1!" } greet "Alice"

5. Function Parameters:

- **Passing Parameters:**

my_function() { local param1=$1 local param2=$2 # Function code using parameters } my_function value1 value2

- **Example (function_parameters_example.sh):**

#!/bin/bash print_info() { echo "Name: $1" echo "Age: $2" } print_info "John" 30

6. Return Values:

- **Using Return Values:**

calculate_sum() { local num1=$1 local num2=$2 local sum=$((num1 + num2)) echo $sum } result=$(calculate_sum 10 20) echo "Sum: $result"

7. Exit Status:

- **Using Exit Status:**

my_function() { # Function code here return 0 # 0 indicates success, non-zero for failure } my_function echo "Exit Status: $?"

8. Recursive Functions:

- **Example (recursive_function_example.sh):**

#!/bin/bash factorial() { if [$1 -eq 0] || [$1 -eq 1]; then echo 1 else local sub_result=$(factorial $(($1 - 1))) echo $(($1 * sub_result)) fi } result=$(factorial 5) echo "Factorial of 5: $result"

9. **Script Best Practices:**

- **Comments:**
- Use comments to explain complex sections.
- **Indentation:**
- Maintain consistent indentation for readability.
- **Error Handling:**
- Implement error checking and handling.
- **Modularity:**
- Break down scripts into functions for reusability.

Shell scripts leverage variables and functions to encapsulate logic, enhance reusability, and organize code efficiently. Understanding how to use variables and create functions is crucial for writing well-structured and maintainable scripts.

- **Automation with Cron Jobs**

1. **Introduction to Cron:**

- **Definition:**
- Cron is a time-based job scheduler in Unix-like operating systems.
- **Crontab:**
- The crontab file contains scheduled tasks for cron.

- **Accessing Crontab:**
- Use the **crontab** command to edit the crontab file.

2. Crontab Syntax:

- **Minute (0 - 59) | Hour (0 - 23) | Day of Month (1 - 31) | Month (1 - 12) | Day of Week (0 - 6):**

```
* * * * * command_to_execute
```

- **Special Characters:**
- * (Wildcard): Matches any value.
- , (Comma): Specifies multiple values.
- - (Hyphen): Specifies a range of values.
- / (Forward Slash): Specifies intervals.

3. Examples of Crontab Entries:

- **Run a Script Every Day at 2:30 PM:**

```
30 14 * * * /path/to/script.sh
```

- **Run a Script Every Monday at 3:45 AM:**

```
45 3 * * 1 /path/to/script.sh
```

- **Run a Script Every Hour:**

```
0 * * * * /path/to/script.sh
```

4. Editing the Crontab File:

- **Edit the Crontab:**

```
crontab -e
```

- **View the Crontab:**

```
crontab -l
```

- **Remove the Crontab:**

```
crontab -r
```

5. Common Cron Job Tasks:

- **Backup:**
- Schedule regular backups of important data.
- **Log Rotation:**
- Rotate and compress log files to manage disk space.
- **System Maintenance:**
- Schedule system maintenance tasks, updates, and cleanup.
- **Automated Reports:**
- Generate and email reports at specific intervals.
- **Database Maintenance:**
- Run database backups and maintenance tasks.

6. Redirecting Output:

- **Send Output to a File:**

0 2 * * * /path/to/script.sh > /path/to/output.log 2>&1

- **Append Output to a File:**

0 2 * * * /path/to/script.sh >> /path/to/output.log 2>&1

7. Environment Variables:

- **Specify Environment Variables:**

SHELL=/bin/bash PATH=/usr/local/bin:/usr/bin:/bin HOME=/path/to/home/directory 0 3 * * * /path/to/script.sh

8. Security Considerations:

- **Limit Permissions:**

- Ensure that the script and its containing directory have appropriate permissions.

- **Use Full Paths:**

- Specify full paths for commands and scripts to avoid path-related issues.

- **Logging:**

- Redirect output to a log file for debugging and monitoring.

9. Troubleshooting:

- **Check Logs:**
- Review system logs and cron logs for any errors.
- **Permissions:**
- Verify that the user running the cron job has the necessary permissions.
- **Environment:**
- Double-check the environment variables and paths.

10. Real-world Examples:

- **Daily Backup Script:**

0 2 * * * /path/to/backup_script.sh

- **Weekly Log Rotation:**

0 3 * * 6 /path/to/log_rotation_script.sh

- **Monthly System Cleanup:**

0 4 1 * * /path/to/cleanup_script.sh

Cron jobs are a powerful tool for automating repetitive tasks, backups, maintenance, and more on Unix-like systems. Understanding the crontab syntax and best practices ensures effective and reliable task scheduling. Regularly review and adjust your cron jobs to meet changing requirements and maintain system efficiency.

CHAPTER 7

ADVANCED LINUX TOPICS

- **Kernel and Device Management**

1. Introduction to the Kernel:

- **Definition:**
- The kernel is the core component of an operating system that manages system resources and provides essential services.
- **Kernel Types:**
- Monolithic, Microkernel, Hybrid.

2. Kernel Modules:

- **Definition:**
- Kernel modules are pieces of code that can be dynamically loaded into the kernel to extend its functionality.
- **Commands:**

lsmod # List loaded modules insmod module # Insert a module rmmod module # Remove a module modprobe module # Insert or remove a module with dependencies

3. Kernel Configuration:

- **Configuration Files:**
- **/boot/config-$(uname -r)**: Current kernel configuration.
- **/usr/src/linux/.config**: Configuration for the kernel being built.
- **Kernel Compilation:**
- **make menuconfig**: Text-based configuration.
- **make xconfig** or **make gconfig**: Graphical configuration.

4. Kernel Parameters:

- **GRUB Configuration:**
- Edit **/etc/default/grub** to modify kernel parameters.
- **Example:**

GRUB_CMDLINE_LINUX="quiet splash"

- **Update GRUB:**

update-grub

5. Device Management:

- **Device Files:**

- Devices in Unix-like systems are represented as files in the **/dev** directory.
- **Major and Minor Numbers:**
- Identify device types and instances.
- **Device Files Creation:**

mknod /dev/device_name c major_number minor_number

6. Device File Types:

- **Character Devices (c):**
- Handle data as a stream of bytes (e.g., terminals, serial ports).
- **Block Devices (b):**
- Handle data in blocks, often associated with storage (e.g., hard drives).
- **Example (mknod):**

mknod /dev/mychardev c 240 0 mknod /dev/myblockdev b 8 0

7. Device Drivers:

- **Definition:**
- Device drivers are kernel modules or parts of the kernel responsible for managing specific hardware devices.
- **Commands:**

lsmod # List loaded modules lspci -k # Display kernel modules for PCI devices lsusb -t # Display USB devices and their drivers

8. udev:

- **Definition:**
- udev is a device manager for the Linux kernel that dynamically creates and removes device nodes.
- **Configuration Files:**
- **/etc/udev/udev.conf**
- Rules files in **/etc/udev/rules.d/**

9. Device File Permissions:

- **Ownership:**
- Device files are typically owned by root.
- **Permissions:**
- Set permissions using **chmod** or udev rules.
- **Example (udev Rule):**

SUBSYSTEM=="usb", ATTRS{idVendor}=="1234", MODE="0666"

10. Hotplugging Devices:

- **Definition:**
- Hotplugging allows the addition or removal of devices while the system is running.
- **Commands:**

echo 1 > /sys/class/scsi_device/device/rescan # Rescan SCSI devices echo 1 > /sys/class/fc_host/host*/issue_lip # Rescan Fibre Channel devices

11. Kernel Panic:

- **Definition:**
- A kernel panic is a critical error from which the operating system cannot recover, requiring a system reboot.
- **Causes:**
- Hardware failures, incompatible kernel modules, corrupted file systems.
- **Recovery:**
- Address the root cause and reboot.

12. System Calls:

- **Definition:**
- System calls are interfaces provided by the kernel that applications use to request services from the operating system.

- **Examples:**
- **open(), read(), write(), ioctl().**

13. Real-time Kernel:

- **Definition:**
- A real-time kernel is designed to provide deterministic response times for certain types of computing tasks.
- **Usage:**
- Critical applications such as robotics, industrial control systems.

Managing the kernel and devices in a Linux system involves configuring kernel options, handling device files, managing modules, and addressing issues like kernel panics. Understanding these aspects is essential for system administrators and developers to maintain a stable and well-functioning Linux environment.

- **Virtualization and Containers (Docker)**

1. Introduction to Virtualization:

- **Definition:**
- Virtualization is the process of creating a virtual instance of a computing resource, such as a server, operating system, storage device, or network.
- **Types:**

- Full virtualization (Hypervisor-based), Para-virtualization, Hardware-assisted virtualization.

2. Hypervisors:

- **Definition:**
- A hypervisor, or Virtual Machine Monitor (VMM), is software or firmware that enables multiple operating systems to share a single hardware host.
- **Types:**
- Type 1 (Bare-Metal): Runs directly on the hardware (e.g., VMware ESXi).
- Type 2 (Hosted): Runs on top of an existing operating system (e.g., VirtualBox).

3. Virtual Machines (VMs):

- **Definition:**
- Virtual machines are isolated instances of an operating system running on a host system.
- **Advantages:**
- Resource isolation, flexibility, and efficient use of hardware.

- **Hypervisors:**
- VMware, KVM (Kernel-based Virtual Machine), Hyper-V.

4. Introduction to Containers:

- **Definition:**
- Containers are lightweight, portable, and isolated environments that package and run applications and their dependencies.
- **Advantages:**
- Resource efficiency, rapid deployment, consistency across environments.
- **Container Runtimes:**
- Docker, containerd, Podman.

5. Docker:

- **Components:**
- Docker Engine, Docker CLI, Docker Compose.
- **Basic Commands:**

docker pull image_name # Pull an image from the Docker Hub docker run image_name # Run a container from an image docker ps # List running containers docker exec -it container_id /bin/bash # Access a running container

6. Docker Images:

- **Definition:**

- Docker images are lightweight, standalone, and executable packages that include everything needed to run a piece of software, including the code, runtime, libraries, and dependencies.

- **Commands:**

docker build -t image_name:tag . # Build an image from a Dockerfile docker images # List available images docker rmi image_name:tag # Remove an image

7. Docker Containers:

- **Definition:**

- Containers are instances of Docker images that run in isolated environments.

- **Commands:**

docker ps # List running containers docker stop container_id # Stop a running container docker start container_id # Start a stopped container docker restart container_id # Restart a container

8. Docker Volumes:

- **Definition:**

- Docker volumes provide a way to persist data generated by and used by Docker containers.

- **Commands:**

docker volume create volume_name # Create a volume docker run -v volume_name:/path/in/container image_name # Mount a volume in a container

9. Docker Compose:

- **Definition:**

- Docker Compose is a tool for defining and running multi-container Docker applications using a YAML file to configure the application's services, networks, and volumes.

- **Commands:**

docker-compose up # Create and start containers docker-compose down # Stop and remove containers docker-compose ps # List running containers in the context of the compose file

10. Docker Networking:

- **Bridge Network:**

- Default network mode for containers, provides isolation.

- **Host Network:**

- Shares the host's network namespace.

- **Overlay Network:**
- Connects multiple Docker daemons, commonly used in swarm mode.

11. Docker Swarm:

- **Definition:**
- Docker Swarm is a native clustering and orchestration solution for Docker.
- **Commands:**

docker swarm init # Initialize a swarm docker swarm join-token worker # Get join token for worker nodes docker service create --replicas 3 image_name # Create a service with three replicas

12. Kubernetes:

- **Definition:**
- Kubernetes is an open-source container orchestration platform for automating the deployment, scaling, and management of containerized applications.
- **Components:**
- Master Node, Worker Node, Pod, Service, Deployment.

- **kubectl Commands:**

kubectl create deployment my-deployment --image=image_name # Create a deployment kubectl get pods # List pods kubectl scale deployment my-deployment --replicas=3 # Scale a deployment

13. Security Considerations:

- **Docker Security:**

- Use official images, minimize image layers, apply least privilege.

- **Container Security:**

- Regularly update and patch containers, implement network segmentation.

- **Kubernetes Security:**

- Secure the Kubernetes API, use RBAC (Role-Based Access Control), encrypt communication.

Virtualization and containerization technologies provide powerful solutions for resource utilization, deployment efficiency, and application isolation. Understanding Docker, container runtimes, and orchestration tools like Kubernetes is crucial for modern development and deployment practices.

- **Filesystem Management and Disk Quotas**

1. **Filesystem Basics:**

- **Definition:**
- A filesystem is a method for storing and organizing files on a storage device.
- **Filesystem Types:**
- ext4, XFS, Btrfs, ZFS.
- **Filesystem Creation:**

mkfs.ext4 /dev/sdX1 # Create an ext4 filesystem mkfs.xfs /dev/sdX1 # Create an XFS filesystem mkfs.btrfs /dev/sdX1 # Create a Btrfs filesystem

2. **Mounting Filesystems:**

- **Mounting a Filesystem:**

mount /dev/sdX1 /mnt # Mount a filesystem

- **Unmounting a Filesystem:**

umount /mnt # Unmount a filesystem

- **Automounting with /etc/fstab:**
- Add an entry in **/etc/fstab** for automatic mounting at boot.

3. **Disk Quotas:**

- **Definition:**

- Disk quotas limit the amount of disk space a user or group can use on a filesystem.
- **Enabling Quotas:**

Edit /etc/fstab and add 'usrquota' and/or 'grpquota' to the mount options /dev/sdX1 /home ext4 defaults,usrquota,grpquota 0 2 # Remount the filesystem mount -o remount /home

4. Quota Commands:

- **Quota Setup:**

quotacheck -cug /home # Create quota files quotaon /home # Enable quotas

- **Checking Quota Usage:**

repquota /home # Display user and group quotas

- **Setting Quotas:**

edquota -u username # Edit user quotas edquota -g groupname # Edit group quotas

5. Soft and Hard Quotas:

- **Soft Quota:**
- Defines a limit, and users are warned when they exceed it.
- Grace period allows users to exceed the limit temporarily.

- **Hard Quota:**
- Defines a strict limit, and users cannot exceed it.

6. Managing Quota Limits:

- **Setting Soft and Hard Limits:**
- Edit the quota file using **edquota**.
- **Example (edquota):**

edquota -u username

7. Quota Exceed Actions:

- **Grace Period:**
- The grace period allows users to exceed their soft limits temporarily.
- **Actions on Quota Exceed:**
- Send warnings, block further disk space allocation.

8. Quota Reporting:

- **Displaying Quota Reports:**

quota -u username # Display user quotas quota -g groupname # Display group quotas

- **Quota Report for All Users:**

repquota /home # Display user and group quotas for all users

9. Disk Usage Analysis:

- **Finding Disk Usage:**

du -h /path # Display disk usage of a directory df -h # Display disk space usage on mounted filesystems

10. Disk Cleanup:

- **Removing Unnecessary Files:**
- Identify and remove unused or large files.
- **Example (Removing Log Files):**

find /var/log -type f -delete

11. Filesystem Maintenance:

- **Filesystem Check (fsck):**
- Check and repair filesystem inconsistencies.

umount /dev/sdX1 # Unmount the filesystem fsck /dev/sdX1 # Check and repair the filesystem mount /dev/sdX1 /mnt # Mount the filesystem back

12. Filesystem Encryption:

- **LUKS (Linux Unified Key Setup):**
- Encrypting entire filesystems or partitions.
- **Commands:**

cryptsetup luksFormat /dev/sdX1 # Format a partition with LUKS cryptsetup luksOpen /dev/sdX1 my_encrypted_volume # Open the encrypted volume

Filesystem management and disk quotas are essential aspects of system administration, ensuring efficient use of disk space and controlling resource usage. Properly configuring quotas and regularly monitoring disk usage contribute to a well-maintained and secure system.

- **High Availability and Clustering**

1. Introduction to High Availability (HA):

- **Definition:**
- High Availability refers to a system or component that is continuously operational for a desirably long length of time.
- **Goals:**
- Minimize downtime, increase reliability.

2. Clustering:

- **Definition:**
- Clustering involves grouping multiple servers or systems together to work as a single logical unit.
- **Types:**

- High Availability Clustering, Load Balancing Clustering.

3. High Availability Clustering:

- **Active-Passive Configuration:**
- One node actively serves, while others remain on standby.
- **Active-Active Configuration:**
- All nodes actively share the workload.
- **Heartbeat Mechanism:**
- Nodes communicate to detect failures.

4. Pacemaker:

- **Definition:**
- Pacemaker is an open-source high-availability resource manager that manages cluster resources, ensuring they are highly available.
- **Resource Agents:**
- Scripts or binaries defining how to start, stop, and monitor resources.
- **Configuration Files:**
- **/etc/corosync/corosync.conf**

- **/etc/pacemaker/crm.conf**

5. Corosync:

- **Definition:**
- Corosync is an open-source project that provides cluster membership and messaging capabilities.
- **Configuration File:**
- **/etc/corosync/corosync.conf**
- **Key Concepts:**
- Nodes, Rings, Quorum.

6. Configuring a Simple HA Cluster:

- **Pacemaker Commands:**

crm configure property stonith-enabled=false # Disable STONITH (Shoot The Other Node In The Head) crm configure primitive my_resource ocf:heartbeat:apache params configfile="/etc/httpd/conf/httpd.conf" op monitor interval="30s" crm configure group my_group my_resource

- **Checking Status:**

crm status

7. Load Balancing Clustering:

- **Definition:**

- Distributes incoming network traffic across multiple servers.
- **Benefits:**
- Improved performance, scalability, and fault tolerance.
- **Common Solutions:**
- HAProxy, Nginx, Keepalived.

8. Keepalived:

- **Definition:**
- Keepalived is a routing software that provides simple and robust facilities for load balancing and high availability.
- **Configuration File:**
- **/etc/keepalived/keepalived.conf**
- **Configuring Virtual IP:**

vrrp_instance VI_1 { state MASTER interface eth0 virtual_router_id 51 priority 100 advert_int 1 authentication { auth_type PASS auth_pass my_secret_password } virtual_ipaddress { 192.168.1.10 } }

9. Distributed File Systems:

- **Definition:**

- A distributed file system allows multiple nodes to share access to files and storage.
- **Examples:**
- GlusterFS, Ceph, Lustre.

10. Quorum in Clustering:

- **Definition:**
- Quorum is the minimum number of votes a distributed system must have to make decisions.
- **Avoiding Split Brain:**
- Ensures there's a majority of active nodes.

11. Monitoring and Alerting:

- **Tools:**
- Nagios, Zabbix, Prometheus.
- **Key Metrics:**
- Resource utilization, node status, cluster health.

12. Disaster Recovery in Clusters:

- **Backup and Restore:**
- Regularly backup cluster configurations.
- **Offsite Replication:**
- Replicate data to a geographically distant location.

13. Documentation and Procedures:

- **Documentation:**
- Maintain detailed documentation of the cluster setup.
- **Procedures:**
- Define procedures for handling failures and maintenance.

High Availability and Clustering are critical components of infrastructure design to ensure continuous operation and fault tolerance. Whether using Pacemaker for HA clusters or tools like Keepalived for load balancing, proper configuration, monitoring, and documentation are essential for maintaining a resilient and highly available system.

- **Linux Certification and Further Learning Paths**

1. **Certifications for Linux Professionals:**

- **CompTIA Linux+ (XK0-004):**
- Entry-level certification covering Linux system administration.
- **Red Hat Certified System Administrator (RHCSA):**
- Demonstrates core skills required for Red Hat Enterprise Linux (RHEL) environments.
- **Red Hat Certified Engineer (RHCE):**

- Advanced certification building on RHCSA, emphasizing advanced Linux skills.
- **LPIC-1: Linux Professional Institute Certification-1:**
- Vendor-neutral certification covering fundamental Linux skills.
- **LPIC-2: Linux Professional Institute Certification-2:**
- Advanced certification focusing on the Linux networking and security.
- **LPIC-3: Linux Professional Institute Certification-3:**
- Senior-level certification offering specialization tracks, such as mixed environment or security.
- **SUSE Certified Administrator (SCA):**
- Certification for SUSE Linux Enterprise Server administrators.
- **SUSE Certified Engineer (SCE):**
- Advanced certification focusing on SUSE Linux Enterprise Server.

2. Online Learning Platforms:

- **Linux Academy:**
- Offers in-depth courses, hands-on labs, and certification preparation.

- **Coursera:**
- Provides Linux courses from top universities and institutions.
- **edX:**
- Offers Linux courses and certifications from universities and industry partners.
- **Udemy:**
- Features a variety of Linux courses, from beginner to advanced levels.

3. Specialized Learning Paths:

- **Linux Kernel Development:**
- Dive into the Linux kernel with resources like "Linux Kernel Development" by Robert Love and kernel development courses on platforms like Pluralsight.
- **Container Orchestration (Kubernetes):**
- Explore Kubernetes with the "Kubernetes: Up and Running" book and courses on platforms like A Cloud Guru.
- **DevOps Practices:**
- Learn about DevOps practices with books like "The Phoenix Project" and courses on platforms like LinkedIn Learning.
- **Linux Security:**

- Strengthen Linux security skills with courses on platforms like Cybrary and Offensive Security certifications like OSCP.

4. Practical Labs and Exercises:

- **Linux Academy Labs:**
- Access hands-on labs for various Linux topics.
- **TryHackMe:**
- Offers Linux-focused capture the flag (CTF) challenges and learning paths.
- **OverTheWire:**
- Provides war games to practice Linux skills, such as "Bandit" for beginners and "Narnia" for more advanced users.

5. Open Source Contributions:

- **GitHub:**
- Contribute to open-source projects and collaborate with the Linux community.
- **Kernel Newbies:**
- Participate in discussions and contribute to the Linux kernel.

6. Books for Further Reading:

- **"The Linux Command Line" by William E. Shotts Jr.:**

- Comprehensive guide to the Linux command line.
- **"UNIX and Linux System Administration Handbook" by Evi Nemeth, Garth Snyder, Trent R. Hein, Ben Whaley:**
- In-depth reference for Linux and Unix system administration.
- **"Linux Pocket Guide" by Daniel J. Barrett:**
- Handy reference for common Linux commands and tasks.
- **"Linux Bible" by Christopher Negus:**
- Comprehensive guide covering various aspects of Linux.

7. Community Involvement:

- **Local Linux User Groups (LUGs):**
- Participate in or start a local LUG to connect with Linux enthusiasts.
- **Forums and Mailing Lists:**
- Join Linux forums and mailing lists to seek help and share knowledge.
- **Conferences and Meetups:**
- Attend Linux conferences and meetups to network and learn from experts.

Continuously expanding your knowledge and skills in the Linux ecosystem involves a combination of certifications, online learning platforms, specialized learning paths, practical labs, open-source contributions, further reading, and community involvement. Stay curious, practice regularly, and engage with the vibrant Linux community to enhance your expertise.

CONCLUSION

In conclusion, diving into the world of Linux offers a vast and rewarding journey for both beginners and experienced professionals. Whether you're aiming to become a certified Linux professional, enhance your skills in specific areas like system administration or security, or contribute to open-source projects, there are numerous resources and learning paths available.

Certifications such as CompTIA Linux+, Red Hat certifications (RHCSA, RHCE), and Linux Professional Institute certifications (LPIC) provide structured paths for skill validation. Online learning platforms like Linux Academy, Coursera, edX, and Udemy offer diverse courses catering to different proficiency levels.

Specialized learning paths, including Linux kernel development, container orchestration (Kubernetes), DevOps practices, and Linux security, allow you to focus on areas aligned with your interests and career goals. Practical labs and exercises on platforms like Linux Academy Labs, TryHackMe, and OverTheWire offer hands-on experiences to reinforce theoretical knowledge.

Active involvement in the open-source community, through contributions on GitHub, participation in forums and mailing lists, and attendance at conferences and meetups, enhances your real-world experience and connects you with fellow Linux enthusiasts.

Books, both comprehensive guides and specific references, provide valuable insights and serve as constant companions on your learning journey. Building a habit of continuous learning, staying engaged with the community, and exploring practical applications of your knowledge contribute to becoming a proficient Linux professional.

In the dynamic and ever-evolving landscape of technology, Linux remains a foundational and integral part. Whether you're exploring Linux for personal curiosity, academic pursuits, or professional advancement, the skills you acquire will undoubtedly empower you in various IT domains. Embrace the challenges, stay curious, and enjoy the process of mastering the Linux operating system.

www.ingramcontent.com/pod-product-compliance
Lightning Source LLC
LaVergne TN
LVHW022228200926
848481LV00006B/2167
* 9 7 9 8 2 2 3 3 2 6 0 4 5 *